How to Prospect and Recruit using Postcards for a MLM or Network Marketing Business

The Low cost Prospecting and Recruiting Tool that Out Performs Online Methods

David Williams

How to Prospect and Recruit using Postcards for a MLM or Network Marketing Business

ISBN 978-1492292371

Table of Contents

Many years ago, when I had only been in Networking for about 2 years, I had reached the top of our pay plan, but knew that success would not stick unless those who helped get me there, my team, found success too. It seemed back then, (and today), that when a prospecting method starts working, it gains traction quickly, and then all you see is that method being used and taught. Soon, it's all you see, and then it dies out from over use.

I'm about to show you a method that won't die out from over use, (yes, I know you THINK you know about postcard recruiting, however as the saying goes 'but you haven't heard about it from me'). Getting back to my story, on how I discovered this method… every 6 weeks or so, another 'leader' from my company came to town.   We leaders who lived in our area acted as hosts, and would do our job and promote him or her, as the next best thing to sliced bread… we promoted the 'event'.

Problem was, each out of town leader seemed to come promoting a different 'recruiting system' that either they used, or worse, sold. Our people would get confused and tried to follow all sorts of different ideas, but could never stick at one long enough to learn to do any of these strategies well, instead, would change course depending on what the next 'fairy dust' sales-pro was selling from the stage.

Frankly I had enough. My key people were having a hard time of it. Old prospecting methods did not work like they once had, and I knew I had to find a way to make prospecting simple again, (not easy, nothing is easy that works, but simple is good).

There was a big conference coming up in Texas, and I needed some time to think. I decided to drive, (nearly 3 days), and NOT answer the phone during the entire drive. Sadly, I arrived at the Texas conference without any new ideas. But it was a nice drive. The event was fantastic, I had a great group there, from all over the US, Canada, and Europe. I was feeling pretty good about that, and many of my team had brought prospects and new folks, so I knew we did business over that weekend. The training was good, the people were excited and the company launched a new product or two.

Soon it was late Sunday afternoon, and the event was nearing its end. I had looked at all the different 'fairy dust' sales pros, and I did not see anything new or interesting that I could use to introduce to my full timers for prospecting. That is when I ran into a fellow leader in my company, hanging around the back of the convention center. I did not know him, nor he me, as we worked on different sides of the country. But he could see from my pin that we were both at the top level, and said hello.

He was a bit like me, he did not behave like he was a rock star, or lead his team like he was a cult leader. I liked to have intelligent, thinking people around me, and he seemed the same. We hit it off right away. Now he was older than I was, and had a very different background. This was my first MLM, and I just seemed to be made for it, I worked hard, and rose to the top of our pay-plan and was earning a lot of money – I did not set any records in my company, but I was doing very well.

One difference between me and other leaders at my position was that I had gone wide, BUT I did not lose old legs as I built new ones. Our pay plan was such that you need to go wide to qualify on your deep business, but many leaders in our company lost their old legs as fast as they built new ones. I really liked my team leaders, and worked with them daily.

FYI, those stair-step compensation plans force you to recruit all the time, so you either learn how, or you quit. Looking back, I know learning to recruit helped me in programs that don't require width, which are much more the norm today. Anyway, he and I retired to an all-night restaurant to talk. My team leaders were all good and hanging out with their team leaders, therefore I was free. He and I went to a 24 hour diner, the kind you might call a 'greasy spoon' but in reality, made great breakfasts 24 hours per day, and poured cup after cup of wonderful fresh coffee.

Because I had worked the business in Europe, he spent a couple of hours grilling me on how to do business there. He wanted to know about what worked, and what did not, cultural differences for marketing, etc. As this book is about postcard recruiting, (and yes, I will get to it), I won't get into how I built the largest team for my company in one country in 9 months, and from there expanded into the rest of Europe… that's for another book.

You have to realize, what I was telling him was about 2 years of trial, error and success over there. He knew that what I was telling him was information one leader normally would not tell another. This was stuff you just shared with your team. But still, I decided to share with him what I knew. However, it was a Quid pro quo, ("this for that" in Latin), and even though we had not said anything about any kind of exchange of information, when I finished my 'Euro Training', and he put his pen down from all the notes he took, I told him my problem. That, in a nut shell, I needed a new mass market prospecting method for full timers.

He sat back, and smiled. He said, 'let me tell you a little about my background'. It turned out that he was one of the top fund raisers for President Bush's election bid. Now, not the kind that has a Rolodex and knows all the wealthy people to call and get a donation. No, he was the kind who did the 'mass market' fund raising of middle class or upper middle class people who may be inclined to help out George.

This guy was one of the best in the world at it, but he only did it for big elections, so while the pay was good, it was only every few years, and only IF he was the one hired and or like the person who wanted to hire him. So, in between elections, he worked our program, using what he knew from the political fund raising business to build his distributorship.

Over the next two hours it was his time to explain what he did. He only had one method to raise money and to recruit for his business. It was the method that worked for raising money for a shot (successfully) at the Presidency, and for reaching the top in our company. It was, of course, what is called Direct Marketing, but in his industry, that meant direct mail marketing.

Now, that in and of itself is nothing new, or not something you could not have thought of on your own. Most of us who end up in networking have thought about mail order as a business idea, or a combination of eBay/Amazon sales/mail order.

Years ago, I remember as a kid seeing some kind of book for sale called 'making money in your underwear' about some guy sitting in his kitchen, without any pants on, making a pile of money at home. It was always advertised for sale in the back of some cheap magazine or comic book. Sadly, my mom would not buy a copy for me. If you are old enough, perhaps you remember the book I am reminiscing about.

But in the days before the Internet, mail order or Direct Mail/Marketing was big. My colleague, who I'll call Ted, explained the process. You needed a targeted list of potential prospects, something to mail, and to take action. As Ted was older than most of us at the level he and I had attained, this approach did not appeal to those of us in the 'younger generation'. This is because most of us used newspaper ads or resume ads. These were ads we could put in the paper one day, and have our phone ringing the next. Sometimes we would have people fax in their resumes, and we would call them back minutes after we got their fax. You see, the point I am making was the short amount of time it took for you to 'take action/place an ad' and have a prospect to talk to.

Place an ad, get calls. It's just like today, 'real time leads', internet leads, which you can buy and get started on quickly. In those days we had offices, meeting rooms, and board rooms. 'Centers' they were called. All of my team of full timers did this method, and it worked, but it worked so well, that all the newspapers eventually had the same ads in them. People would call your ad, and say 'I think I already have an interview with your company'.

Success is not always good thing. Too many people doing the same thing, and the process gets saturated. 20 people placing ads in 3 papers in one city DOES make a program look saturated, and does no one any good.

Now I was pretty clever and would come up with new ads for my team to use, until the rest of the pack copied me, and eventually so would other MLM companies. So, I could see the writing on the wall as far as ads in big city papers, and realized that this method could not continue, but I had to find a replacement way for my full timers to fill their appointment calendars. I needed another mass marketing recruiting or prospecting method.

If you are wondering if this ramble down the history of MLM should mean anything to you, well, I can only say that perhaps you can't relate to parts of this story, except for this one area: I was in a situation just like you are today, I had no way to mass market prospect. The reason may be different - you are not prospecting via newspaper ads like I did. No, you are using 'internet leads'. But be honest. Most of the leads you buy from lead generation companies are crap. The prospects are not there when you call, or they can't even remember being interested in a home based business.

Perhaps that is not your prospecting problem, but if you are in a situation where you have no prospects (in terms of mass recruiting which is all I am talking about here) then we have that in common, and hence, it is in your interest to know just how important learning the Direct Mail prospecting and recruiting method is. It's important because it's different.

FYI – this is not about those yellow pre-printed tacky MLM postcards. (Forgive me if I say that again later!) One day I will write the book on everything else I learned about direct mail recruiting, but for now I am going to only focus on postcards, because they are the least expensive, and the fastest for you to get going, besides being one of the most effective of the direct marketing methods. And let me just say here, that my postcard methods is NOT at all like any of those others, as you will find out soon. In fact, it is very much contrary to the training and methods postcard 'gurus' teach.

The difference is, I don't sell postcards, or leads etc., so I'm giving you the methods that work, without any backend to me.

Now, back to Ted. Ted explained what he did to reach the top in our company. He said that it took time to set up and work, but it worked very well. It was also duplicateable.

Interestingly, one of the downsides of the time when newspaper ads worked, was the fact that people who joined your team from an ad only wanted to do ads. No matter what you told them about warm market, etc., they would want to put in the same ad in the paper the following week that triggered them to join. Of course, new distributors were a disaster on the phone and lost all the callers, wasting the ad and the prospect.

By the way, I learned a stratagem to deal with this, and I'll tell it to you now, as I applied it to my postcard recruiting – with the exception that it worked even better! – For those new distributors who wanted to place ads, I would have them place their ad in the paper, but with MY phone number, and their name in the ad. Any call that came into my office asking for Mr. X, I knew was a potential prospect for my new guy. It worked well, as in that pay plan, if it was my recruit, I earned most if not all of the commission from that ad until my new guy qualified at a higher volume level. Something else I learned: when I ran into someone who wanted to join without buying any products, I would suggest this idea to him, and from that day on I rarely had to pay 'out of pocket' for my advertising. In those day's ads would cost about $300 per week – these were professional looking ads in cities of over a few million people.

Back when Ted was doing his direct mail recruiting, some people (like me) had personal computers, but there was no Internet as we know it. I was a computer geek (sort of) so I knew about word-processing and mail merge - where you could type up one letter, load in a file of names and address, press print and your printer would spit out personalized letters to all of the names on your list. Of course, this is nothing today, but back then it impressed recipients, because a lot of people figured you had to still type a letter by hand, and assumed that the letter was personalized, and therefore it was much more meaningful.

Still, Ted knew that the typewriter age was over and more and more people knew about form letters, but he had a few tricks. On his letters, he added a personalized post it note, you know, those sticky little square (usually yellow) pieces of paper that stick to other paper? Well, he would write something on it, with the receivers first name, and sign it, something like; 'Bob, I'm telling you this works, call me today, Ted' and stick it on the lower third of the letter, that way it would be seen when the addressee first opened it.

You know what? Ted told me that post it note was the first thing that was read by people opening the letter. He reveled a lot of things, too much to explain here, but the reason I mention the post it note, was because of the hand written part. No matter if you knew the letter was printed by a computer or not, you knew the post it note was real and hand-written.

Over the next 10 years, I learned more and more about Direct Mail MLM recruiting, by talking to Ted, and by testing and testing after Ted retired. There is no one perfect way for Direct Mail to work, there are lots of great methods, but for the purpose of this discussion, I will divide MLM direct mail into two types: postcards and other. This book will just cover postcards, the perfect way to do it, and a lot of little strategies and tactics to save you time, get your mailings for nearly free, and to build up your MLM empire.

So, why did I tell you all of this history? Because I wanted to send home two important messages, 1) I learned from an expert, and now you are too, and 2) the trick, or the reason that this works, is we combine personalizing with mass prospecting.

Anyone can do one-on-one prospecting, but if you can master mass prospecting that is personalized, and have your team doing it too, you will earn a fortune quickly and have a solid team not dependent on rubbish 'online leads'.

OK? So are you ready to say yes to learn 'Mass Marketing Personalized Direct Mail Postcard Recruiting'? (Can you tell I used to teach this in seminars where my clients paid over 10K for the weekend?)

Now, I'm going to break down this training into 3 parts:

1)   the physical postcard

2)   the list – who you'll be sending the cards to

3)   the message – what to say on the card

You will find a lot of nuggets of wisdom and ideas in each part.

Why a postcard?

Back in the olden days people sent letters and postcards to each other. They went on vacations and took pictures that had to be developed later at home. In order to make friends and family jealous of where they spent these vacations, they bought postcards and sent them to coworkers. Long ago, people got lots of mail, mostly from people they owed money too, and a few letters from aunts and uncles who would not pay the high cost of calling long distance.

Funny, apart from the bills, people enjoyed getting mail; letters and cards.

Then came the Internet. Email, texting, Facebook, Skype, who writes letters anymore? Few of us even get paper utility bills or monthly credit cards statements. If you do, you pay extra. I know. I save $2 per statement if I elect to get them via email instead, which I do. With the advent of the Internet, it was the end of a lot of Direct Mail companies and the end of sending out cards and letters.

Sure, there are companies, some MLM that just sell cards! You pick a card from their website, and provide an address and a message, and a real card is sent out to the person of your choice. Of course, once the person opens the card, the illusion of personalization is over, but it was nice for the few seconds it lasted. It's just a hand-written font, and it fools no one.

The fact that no one sends REAL mail, letters or cards, is the reason why prospecting and recruiting through postcards work. Now, let me say one thing right here and now:

THIS IS NOT A TRAINING ABOUT SENDING 'OPPORTUNITY' TYPE YELLOW CARDS, CARDS WITH MONEY OR FANCY CARS OR UGLY, CRASS TACKY PICTURES WITH SPAMMY MESSAGES WITH AN ADDRESS LABEL STUCK ON THE CARD!

No, I am going to teach you a way to mass recruit, in an assembly line fashion, with personalized Picture postcards. And for the record, the postcard is real, i.e. a card with a nice picture of something/place.

First WHY it works.

If you send a spammy yellow 'recruiting' opportunity card, it gets glanced at for a second, and trashed. Unless you are someone who thinks ugly tacky cards are good, you trash it. As a MLM (retired) person myself, when I get those, I just shake my head sadly, and wonder what kind of person would actually LIKE a card like that? With their name stuck on the card by a label. Really?

Is that the kind of person that you feel would be your company's next $100,000 per month earner? Really?

Sadly, there are postcard reports and trainings on the net that suggest this is a good method. However, they are selling you cards or other MLM systems, etc. Forget these crappy and tacky ugly cards, you are going to learn how to do magic and recruit good quality people who will actually be impressed with your card system. Some will join just because of it.

Picture this.

Imagine you have a dull job. You come home after work and you go and look at your mail. Among the bills, if there are any, is a real postcard. You look at the photo, and you see it's of a nice vacation place, or perhaps the Statue of Liberty. Now, what do you do next? You flip the card to the other side to see who it's from. First thing you do is look at the signature. You don't read the message first, you look to see who it's from. It's says it's from 'Peter'. You don't remember a Peter, so you double check to see if it is addressed to you. It is.

So now you read the message to see if you can figure out who Peter is.

You just got your prospect to just READ your message.

They read your message!!! You actually had someone read your 'junk' mail! That is considered a major achievement in the corporate world of direct mail.

Now, it's important to note, that the entire postcard was hand written. Name, address, message and signature. There is a real stamp on the card too.

OK, before you roll your eyes that is too much writing, listen to me, you are not going to handwrite these cards yourself, nor are you going to outsource this writing.

Here is part of the magic. You are going to have the message, and your signature printed in black, in your handwriting, on each card.

What's that again?

Here is what you will do.

First, you need to buy postcards.

If you live in a large city, check the net for listings of postcard printers/wholesalers in your area. Most of my MLM life has been in big cities, so I would just find a local postcard printer or wholesaler, drive over and make a deal for some old stock. Often there are postcards that seem out of date that retailors don't want. For example, downtown shots where there is now a new building, or perhaps just some that are not selling well. These are just fine for our purpose.

Buy in bulk, you should not pay more than 10 cents per card, because 10 cents is what you will pay for them retail at a dollar store. You can also look online for wholesalers, if there are none in your area. Call them, don't order online. When you call, ask for old or returned, or out of date stock. They will make a deal with you. It really is not that important what the image is, as long as it appears to be a real postcard, (i.e. not some picture that appears as advertising). It needs to look like a post card. Don't buy the oversized kind, and if you can get the really small kind, you can pay less postage often when mailing it. It will depend on what country you live in. Here in the U.S. there is a postcard rate for smaller postcards, so look into that in your country. Usually you can find out online.

Now, if you have a budget of a few hundred dollars, buy a lot of cards, because you will be reselling them to your team, as you build and recruit them. Most people want to have systems laid out for them, so you will need a couple of thousand cards, as you will provide 250 to 500 to each new member.

If you are on a low or no budget program, you can purchase your cards at dollars stores. Typically these cards cost you ten cents, especially if you buy 10 or more at a time. Don't just go to the first dollar store you find if they are trying to sell them to you for .25 cents each. Look around. If you can't find them then look online, I would hate to see anyone pay more than a dime (ten cents). If the dollar store owner is there, speak to him about getting some deal. If not, Google is your friend, search and you will find discounted stock.

Be sure all the cards you get are the same, or if not the same, are the same size and have the same backside. Usually there is a line down the middle, a square where a stamp should go, a description of what the image is, and some copyright on the bottom. You need to be sure all the cards you purchase have the same backside orientation.

Next step is to go to your local office store, (Office Max, or some such store), and get a nice BLACK roller ball pen. This is a pen that writes like a magic marker, but you want it to be thin tipped. Not thick, not medium, but thin. There is a reason for this, which I will explain soon.

Now, go home and take a piece of nice white bond paper. Have a copy of your message ready. Now tape a postcard to your kitchen table, image facing the table. Tape it so it lays flat. Now take an 8.5 x 11 inch bond paper and tape it over the postcard. You should be able to see the postcard through the paper.

With your new black roller ball thin pen, write your message on the white paper, and your signature, (don't worry about the message for now, the text is covered in the last chapter). What you are doing is creating a template of YOUR hand written text positioned so it will can be printed in your hand-writing by a professional quick printer.

Armed with your 8.5 x 11 inch template and your box of postcards, go to your local quick printer. I usually don't use Office Max for this, but you can try. Some can and some can't. Sometimes it is because they are not really trained on how, as often they are just kids who learn how to use a fancy photocopier. So, go to a quick printer, and they will look at what you have and know what to do. It's very easy, and the finished result is perfect.

When you get them back, you will have all your postcards with your hand-written message, and your signature appearing as if you just wrote the card yourself. Many times printers were amazed at how good the quality is.

It's so good, that I have had people call me from all over the world wondering how I did this, they could tell the address and their name were hand written, because they were unique, and assume the message was too. Once your printer hands you back your cards, proceed home and think about what movie you want to watch.

Why?

Because now you are going to hand address each card. Yes, it's a little work, but not too much. I told my downline, 'look, one evening per week, just find something on Netflix to watch, (or whatever you like on TV), and take your list, and write out each card'. Most of the work is done for you. Your list (don't worry, we will get to lists in another chapter), will have your prospects contact information, so you will write their first name above the message on the left side of the card, and their full name and address on the right side. And while you are doing this, you are enjoying some (quality) time with your spouse watching TV. I'm such an old timer networker that I still don't have TV, but I do watch movies on my computer, and have a 55 inch TV that I use as a monitor. I guess I should say I have no cable. I am reminded of the old Amway saying 'there's no PV in TV'. I've never been in Amway, but there is no money to be made watching TV, unless you're addressing postcards!

Side note: Once you have set this up, as a system, and have too many leads to deal with, I suggest you only send 10 cards per day. Forget having to watch movies, because addressing ten cards does not take too long. I would just sign at my desk and address them while I made calls. For example, when I was on hold, or waiting for a prospect to come to the phone, as you will find that addressing 10 cards takes very little time. My entire team did 10 cards per day each, as did those who joined us who were recruited by postcard. That's leverage!

One day I was in Paris, attending a big opportunity meeting. It was an open meeting, and a lot of the room were members of my team. I was not part of the meeting, I was just there supporting. The person who closed the meeting asked some of the new people in the room to stand up, and then he asked them how they heard of XYZ Company, expecting to hear about 'warm market'. 40% answered that they got a nice postcard from their sponsor. I knew keen members of other downlines were pondering what that meant.

So you see, most of the work is done by the printer. You do have to address the cards, because the message in your handwriting has to match the name and address – that is the magic.

By now, some smart guy reading this is thinking 'I guess the author doesn't know about hand written fonts'. Come on, of course I do, but people know real writing when they see it. My mother says I have the hand writing of a serial killer, (joke), the point is, it looks real. If you are going to outsource this, (and I have from time to time), find a local person you can hire who has nice hand writing. If you are a guy, use a guy, and vice a versa for women. People can tell the difference. Don't use hearts to dot the 'i', or any non-business like writing style. Friendly, readable, and clear. Not too small either, for two reasons: 1) when the postcard is printed the text enlarges just a tiny bit, hence me telling you to use a thin roller ball pen, and second, if you write too small, your message will appear to not be long enough. Practice writing it out a few times to get the right size on your template.

If you use a hand-written font, you won't have used the magic, and your results will suffer.

Once you have your postcards addressed, it's time to put a stamp on them. Depending on your country, and postal service, see if you can find some interesting stamp. Sometimes you need a small stamp if you do write the address too large, and that's fine, however, if you have room, always find a stamp that is different or interesting. I know there are some that are self-sticking or have self-adhesive, again, those are fine, but I have found the best results with stamps that were not the common variety. Remember, you are making this mailing look 'personal' and that means using a stamp that does not look as if it was the same kind used by a business, i.e. the set stamp for your postage rate. Sometimes you need to go to a larger post office to get these stamps, but it's worth it.

After that, you can take your finished cards to your local post office to mail, this will get them off faster than just tossing them into your local mail box. I usually mail one to myself at the same time, just so I know when they may start hitting prospects. Even if you are mailing all over the country send one to yourself, when you cards arrives, you know the rest are sure to follow in the next few days.

Here is where you can do well, or do poorly.

In the U.S. there are so many mailing lists for sale and rent, it's not funny. When I work the business in other countries, it becomes more difficult. Still, if you are NOT in the U.S., I have found lists in Canada, and in the major European countries. The non-U.S. nations just don't (yet) have a lot of 'opportunity seekers' or 'home based business' buyers lists yet. So you have to see their catalog of lists to make an educated guess. Reading my section below on horizontal lists will be a big help.

In the U.S. we have so many options, which becomes the problem. I have only tried MLM opportunity seekers one time, and never again. It was a cheap list, and I wasted my time and money on the postage. Now, you may find some of these lists that are good, and if you have tested or used them (or they are so cheap that you want to test a couple of hundred postcards on them), or you trust your list broker, then fine. However, I don't recommend them.

Horizontal lists

Think outside the box. That is what I mean by horizontal lists. I realize that many trainers and lead sellers say get MLM lists, because they are people looking to join an MLM. However, but I have found this group one or all of the following: cheap, jaded, looking for you to do everything for them, or they enter the witness protection program faster than you can say NEXT. Rather than go after this group, I suggest you look at a horizontal group, those looking to make money from home, or to make money, but not through MLM. Often these people all know about MLM, and have been in some, but have found that whatever one they joined did not work for them. So they are trying something else.

For example, I like to buy lists of people who tried day-trading, bought options courses, Forex training, mail order business, eBay or other home based business that require some investment. This means the list I buy or rent are people who are intelligent, have money, willing to study and take the time to learn. They are not the MLM junkies which I find make up the MLM lists. This group tend to make slower decisions, which leads to a longer series of exposures, (of which we will discuss later).

Another group to look at are those who have spent money on vitamins (or nutritional products, books, etc.) This is of course if you have some kind of wellness MLM program, but be sure you find a list where they spend money, not just added their name for information. I know that a 'spent money' list is more expensive, but at the end of the day it's far cheaper, because you close more business.

Weight loss is another group. It's a pretty big group in the U.S. where everyone seems to be on a diet, but once again, find people who spend money. If you are in a program that connects to 'working out' you can find a list of men's and women's fitness magazines, buyers of protein products, etc. If you look at the different lists that are offered, and think about each type of person on that list, you can figure out who best to target.

At this point, let me get to something that prospects will ask you during the prospecting process, usually as part of your first conversation with them: "Where did you get my name?" This is a common question (although it is becoming less and less common as people know they end up on lists), and I used to tell them I got their name from 'Liz Brown' because she was my list broker, (many lists are sold or rented by list brokers), which was true. I did get their name from her, (or whoever gave me the list). Those in my downline were told to say they got their name from me. Which was all so true.

However, I later learned a better strategy. Now we answer the question 'Where did you get my name with…

'That is proprietary information. As I said, we are looking to build a big team, and those who become part of the team have access to where we get all of our contacts, including the sources of people, like yourself, who are willing to spend a few hours a week part time to earn an extra $4000 per month, or more. Should you start working with us all of our proprietary strategies will be shared with you. Now, I just want to remind you, this information is particular to 'team name' only, it's not something each XYZ distributor has access to'.

You are selling the value of joining YOUR TEAM.

The Challenges with Lists

Some lists have no terms, or simple terms; you buy names, or you rent names. If you buy the names you can do what you like with the list, mail them once, twice, or 100 times. If you rent a list however, you have terms. Like only mailing to the list once, and often showing them what you want to mail first. When we started in Direct Mail, we mailed out letters that were pretty dull on color letter head and the letter was always approved by the list broker/owner. Postcards at first were held back, as it was a new concept, but now it is no longer new. All I suggest is this: when a broker or list owner asks for a sample mail piece, give them one that is NOT handwritten. (This is not a trick or dishonest, there is no rule against this, it's just because I found it held things up, so email your message, and provide them a blank card, saying the message will go on the post card. You can even just scan a blank card too, front and back, and email it to them. This will get you approved faster, and without risk.

You may be wondering why? Well, we live in a world of complainers, and those trying to protect their jobs. A list broker must pass the mail shot (the mail piece) to the company you are renting the list from. This could be a magazine and they have their 'image' to consider. A hand written post card might not look right to some non-MLM savvy blow-hard in the corporate magazine culture. So, scan a card, and email the message to your broker and you will have few if any challenges. You do NOT have to mention that the card will be hand written etc.

How do list companies know if you cheat and mail more than one time? When you get your names, you usually get more than you pay for. Which is nice, but it's also because a list renter will 'seed' the list with a few phony names but with real home addresses of some of their staff. I got so good at reading lists I could often find these. How? I'll tell you in a minute. So, if you try to mail out to the list more than one time, you will be caught. It's not something I would do anyway, because while it is true that you get more success on the 3rd to 8th mailing, it is too expensive to do. It may happen by mistake if you are giving downline different parts of your list, but be careful and track your list so it won't happen. You will be better off with a new list then a repeat mailing to an old list, because there are many on the list who will start right away in your program.

And if you do things the way I suggest, you will have access to these prospects via the phone. You will also find that people keep your card for a long time, and then call your message/and or you later. In the past, I always called people on the phone after I sent them my card. It does not say in the list terms that you can't do this, but I don't recommend that you tell them you plan to. Remember, you usually don't get the phone number with the lists, but what I would do is sit on the computer and look up each name.

That was how I could spot a 'seed', sometimes I could tell because I had seen that address before with a different name as some lists were seeded by people with little imagination.

When I worked a list, I would not even mail out to those without phone numbers, because I wanted to call those I mailed to. Sometimes I would mail the non-phone number list after I was finished that campaign, or let downline without any prospects or much money take them for the cost of the stamps. You see, calling someone and saying 'did you get my post card last week' usually brought a positive answer, 'yes, what was that all about anyway?'

Now my message back then was different, and I don't do out call campaigns as much anymore, but if you have the phone numbers, it's a great opening line, 'did you get my postcard'. That line works very well, but not all new recruits are as comfortable to call as you might be, so that is why I stopped doing it as much. Still, it's powerful. It opens the conversation, and I never any negativity on the phone. Some were not interested, of course, or asked 'where did you get my name' but typically there was interest, and we got 20 to 30 per cent of people we called to a meeting or one on one presentation. Getting them on webinars is even easier!

More info on Lists

In some cases you can rent lists with phone numbers, depending on the list. If you can do this, I would if it is in your budget. Remember, consider what your average new recruit product purchase is, and your profit on that purchase. You want your program to be more than self-funding, you want it to be profitable. Of course, as your downline grows and builds you will earn many times over the initial profit on the first purchase, but there is also the attrition factor, people do join, do nothing, and leave, so factor in your costs.

When you are speaking with a list owner or broker, and it's a big list, feel free to tell them you want to test the list. For example if a list is 150,000 in size, say you want to test 5000 or 10,000 depending on how many of your team you can subdivide the list with. If you have 10 people in your team, you should be able to get them to take a 1000 names each, or 500 minimum. Some really crafty list owners will provide you with the best names on their list for the test, hoping you will come back for the rest. They will give you 5000 or 10,000 of the best buyers, which does give you an edge, because you can use this list, and then test again with another order of the same size. If the result is not as good as the first time, you know what your broker is doing.

If you want to be crafty, order a test of a different list, and hope you get the best buyers again on the new list, or, don't take chances, find a new list owner/broker and explain what the old one did, (so they know you are on to their games).

Other ways to get lists

Trades. Once you have bought a list, and worked it, it is great to trade with a horizontal company for their list. Most magazines, health clubs, etc., DON'T have the same 'we don't rent, or sell your name to anyone' that a basic opt-in email form has. In fact they sell, rent and trade your name often. It's called database marketing, and it's normal. You can do it on a smaller level. For example, if you have bought a list of buyers of 'X' for all of one city, (let's say you find a big list, and you live in a fair sized city, so you tell the list provider I want all your list of 'vitamin buyers or nutritional product buyers for Chicago', because you live in Chicago, and have local meetings there for your program.

Now, if you are looking to do long distance sponsoring, which works just fine with postcard don't worry, I will get to that, but read this example as it may get you thinking about trades.

Your list broker says 'we only have 5500 names in Chicago', so you tell them fine, you'll take it, and try another city or state later. In this example you buy the list. Once you have worked the list, you can look for non MLM business that could use your list. There are many; local gyms, local health food stores, local health magazines, etc. that could use your list for their marketing. You can look up more on a google local search. Call them and tell them what list you have, and explain you are looking to trade lists, name for name. You can do this over and over, building up your own database.

MLM lists or Genealogies

Genealogies of MLM companies get swapped around, and you can buy them often of companies that are out of business. While this seems like the best list, in my experience they are out of date, filled with people who did nothing, and give you the least bang for your buck. I had a few that I got from time to time that I would trade, but I would never spend any more money mailing to them. I suggest you spend good money to get a good list and avoid genealogies.

Co-op your costs

For those of you on a low to no budget, here is a strategy for you. Find the cost of a good list, perhaps it's going to be a few hundred dollars, much more than you have to spend, and you don't need 5000 names now, as you are by yourself, (5000 is often a minimum), here is what to do:

First take inventory. Do you have ANY downline? Even a dead distributor can be woken up if you offer them a method. Most distributors quit because they can't 'do the business' i.e. find people to sponsor. Sometimes they are smart people who thought they did not need any help and found that none of their business buddies wanted to have anything to do with your program. These are perfect people to see. Go to them, give them a copy of the paperback version of this book, or just a good overview of your business plan based on the book, including all the costs. If you have 3 people like this you will be able to afford your list. Not only that, you now have 3 people in your team prospecting with a system.

You see, using a system is better than no system. The more time you and your team invest in one system, the better and better you get at it. And soon you get new people to join from the system who only want to use the same system, and by that time you sound like an expert and they quickly follow your lead.

Ok, so, let's say you are sitting by yourself, no downline, and not enough money to buy or rent 5000 names. What do you do? You go back to people who said 'no' to you. Trust me, many of those who said no to you said no because they felt they did not have any system to prospect from, and were not interested in 'buying leads', (those crappie leads that are sold online). Present your marketing plan to these people, (you can show this book, or show them postcards), explain the list you are going to rent or buy, and recruit yourself a team. You don't even have to find people who 'buy' products, as long as they join and pay their share of the list cost. There are a lot of lazy and cheap people out there looking for what they think is an easy solution to work, and if they think postcards are it, well, let them pay to play, at least you get your list.

Postcards are not easy, but they are simple. And the method I teach works better and with a higher rate of success then the use of traditional tacky MLM opportunity label postcards. By a huge margin! You will find success rapidly this way.

In any event, recruit 5 people who only have to come up with their share of the cost of the list fee, and you have your list paid for. If you do this method, and I have, follow up, and work the leads and names of those new recruits of yours, there is a good chance they don't follow up, and as you are their direct sponsor, you can still sign up any one who joins direct to them, but still get paid on new product orders, (in typical compensation plans). All I am saying is to follow up on all cards sent if you don't trust some of your team. There are people on that list waiting for you to reach out to them. This means just keep a watchful eye on people who join only because of the lead program.   If it looks like they are too into TV, offer to follow up on their leads for them. You'll find the right person sooner or later to replace your lazy downline.

The Message

At this point, I want to cover a bit of marketing and copywriting basics, that will explain why we use the type of messages I am about to show you.

First - which I hope you know by now – is to understand the principle of 'recruiting is a process not an event'. This means we don't try to explain everything about our business, products and compensation plan in one message and add the immortal lines of 'well, what do you think?' all in one go.

No, remember the basics of what we are doing.

1.   We use a 'handwritten' postcard to ensure your message gets read.

2.   Our message is only to get the prospect to take the next exposure step

So, our message must only interest the person enough to take the next step, in a positive and pro-active way.

Let me tell you now, if you have the idea that you could create a website that had a recorded opportunity call, pages about the products, some training and a call to action with a link to your replicated company website 'sign up form' - forget it. Many novices have tried this, and died. People need to be 'courted' – it's a process – helped along the way – via a series of exposures.

I'm writing this so you know that it is NOT a good idea to try and compose a message that will take someone from reading the card to going direct to your sign up page, forget that, that's dreamland.

Postcards are a prospecting tool, and that is why you bought this book, because you lack prospects, so don't expect postcards to be able to convince your prospect to do anything more than take the next step, (which we will cover).

What is your next step?

Depending on how you wish to go at this point will determine your message somewhat. Here are some choices:

1.   Have your prospect call you

2.   Have your prospect call a 24 hour voice mail message (2 to 4 minutes)

3.   Have your prospect call a 24 hour GAP line message 8 to 12 minute presentation

4.   Have your prospect go to a web site

Now, unless you are just perfect on the phone, I don't suggest you follow 'have your prospect call you'. Even if you are perfect on the phone, your prospect is not, and knows he or she can't duplicate your method. For that reason alone, I don't like the first option.

The second option, that they listen to short message is, in my opinion, the best. If your message on the postcard promises something of value, (as determined by your message), that can be obtained from your recorded message, you will have promised something and delivered, your prospect will keep seeing more from you.

The third option is a long message, called a GAP line, (GAP stands for 'grab a pen'), and it's really a mini opportunity presentation. The best use of a GAP line is AFTER you have spoken to someone. Typically, it works like this:

Prospect listens to short message, reads an ad, online or other, watches a short online video, but has zero info, he is just excited or interested to learn more. They call you or you call them, and now they are on the phone with you, and they are ready to find out from you 'about your X'. You have asked them a few questions, but they are now at the point of expecting something from you.

You say: 'Ok Bob, look, I've asked you enough questions and you seem to meet the requirements I'm looking for/we seem like a good fit/you sound serious, (you are saying something nice about the prospect and as a reward you are now going to provide what he wants to know), so let me get to how we are making $10K a month here/$4k a month here/losing weight so fast but without any side effects/(or whatever your main selling benefit is to the prospect), now pause for just half a second, as if you are taking in a breath, and continue with, 'have you go about 10 minutes right now?'

Say nothing until your prospect answers.

Typically they say yes, if they say yes, say: 'Great, grab a pen', (wait until they indicate they have a pen – often they need a minute – say nothing until they are ready) 'take this number down, xxx-xxx-xxxx, it's a 10 minute recorded presentation that covers A to Z all the (fill in your core benefit/message etc.). Be sure to sell it as the answer – as it is the answer – to his question of 'what is it all about'. Now say this 'I'll call you back in 11 minutes and we can take it from there, I think it will be a perfect fit for you, but if not, just let me know, and that's ok too. Can you read that number back to me? Great, talk to you in 11, bye.'

Now your prospect just said they had 10 minutes, so they can't back out, and you have done two things: put your prospect on a professional presentation, (which he can't interrupt with questions if he tried), and two, you showed him, (you may have to explain this to him), how duplicable this process was, i.e. he could do what you just did.

Call you prospect back in the allotted time, if they don't answer, wait a bit and try again. If they don't like it, they will avoid your call, or just answer and tell you 'No', and you can move on. If they answer with questions, take them to the next step because you now have a REAL prospect.

If they say they don't have 10 minutes now, set up a time for you to re-connect when they do. DON'T give out the 10 minute GAP line number and say call it later. Don't, even mention it. Find out when they have more time and end the call.

Call them back at the right time and use the script properly.

Option 3 will provide you with better prospects, for a prospect who reads your postcard, calls and listens to your long GAP line message for ten minutes and leaves his name and number is very interested. The challenge is that the message on the card must sell a 10 minute commitment rather than a 2 minute one. This is harder to do, and will leave a lot of good people not calling you. However, the advantage is that you don't have to speak to as many people, so you do less work. So, like most of life, less work, easier systems produce less results. If you have the money, and just want to talk to those who are really interested, its fine to use this system, you just have to mail out more cards.

Fourth and last option – the Web site.

This is the easiest method to do but it achieves 'easy' results, (meaning poor results). Why? Mostly because someone walks into their home with a real postcard, (it's REAL, not virtual). They are more likely to pick up their landline, and call your number, than walk to a computer, turn it on, wait for it to warm up while they sort through what other things they came home with or arrived in the mail. If they put your postcard down, chances are they get sidetracked when they hit their home page. Perhaps they notice incoming email, Facebook messages, etc. You have now directed them to a device (their computer) connected to a large assortment of time wasting and distracting activities (the Internet), and perhaps lost your prospect...

Maybe later they will re-read your card and type your site into their address bar, but trust me, as they do that, they have other windows open, are monitoring Facebook status, Skype messages, and have iTunes playing it the background. No matter how good your site is, it's pretty hard to compete with everything else on the net, UNTIL they know there are reasons for them to visit your great site. Now, that will come but not until after a continued series of exposures, (like the systems above).

So, if you are really lazy, and really have lots of cash, try the website method, and you'll get some people, I'm sure, you will just get so many more if you use the method I have found to work the best, method 2, - have your prospect call a 24 hour voice mail message (2 to 4 minutes). But in the end, it's up to you.

The Actual Message

There are 5 parts to the message, you can mix up the bodies, change the opening lines, etc., so we will cover the areas, and then give you the actual text.

1.   Salutation – I don't like to use 'Dear' just because when you hand write it, it seems too personal, in the sense that someone is dear to you. I like the informal 'Hi'. Word Count: 2

2.   Opening Line – Promise – Attention Getter – Benefit – whatever you call it, this line is important – as it gets the rest of the postcard read. Word Count: (for 2 and 3 together is 33 words average for smaller card, nearly the same for larger card)

3.   Main Body (includes Opening Line). Word Count: see above for total

4.   From – this is you – I like to put – Dave (David Williams) another example could be: Mary (Mary Higgins) Word Count: 1 to 3

5.   Call to Action - Word Count: (for smaller card 10 words, for larger 16)

Now, you might think that smaller word counts are easier to write messages for then longer word counts, but they are not. However, don't try and cram in more words, and, if you write small, try to write larger, to fill the space. You don't want your message to look crammed or left with lots of white space either.

I'm going to give you a few examples that you can use, all of them work, but you will see the pattern and find it simple to adapt for your program or product. Some speak about making money or finding success, which can be your upline's, or team mates success, or you can adapt to your own earnings. That part is up to you, as I don't know your situation, but I know it's going to get better.

Lots of people in MLM are happy with their company or product, they just can't recruit. They have no system to make that happen. If you can show them a system, they will follow you in your company. That's why 'finding leads' and this 'method' are good subjects of the postcards.

However, I have provided you with examples for 'leading with the product' as well as other opportunity type messages.

Have you given up on networking over lack of leads? I've found a new access to 1000's of prospects – all off-line. Mary, this is working for me! How? Call me at 212 234 3234 to hear a 2 min message and I'll tell you this secret. It works! (or Call Now!)

$4289 or more per month in MLM. Finally I have a simple offline lead system that works. Mary, I'm making money. Full details - Call me at 212 234 3234 to hear a 2 min message revealing this secret. It works! (or Call Now!)

You can replace 'Mary, I'm making money' with 'Mary, we're making money' or 'Mary, people are calling us to join'

After x years I have finally cracked the MLM code. It's all about getting leads, nothing to do with the internet! Call me at 212 234 3234 to hear a 2 min message to learn how I cracked it! It works! (or Call Now!)

Forget trying to make money online. How about $X per month? Really. Call me at 212 234 3234 to hear a 2 min message revealing this secret. It works! (or Call Now!)

Forget trying to make money online, I've finally learned how to make MLM work for me. Call me at 212 234 3234 to hear a 2 min message and I'll share with you this secret. It works! (or Call Now!)

I've finally found a MLM system that works. We've recruited over 181 people so far– and it's nothing to do with the internet! Call me at 212 234 3234 to hear a 2 min message revealing this secret. It works! (or Call Now!)

I really have found a way to earn over $xxx per month. Really. This is working for me and it's amazing. Call me at 212 234 3234 to hear a 2 min message outlining how I do it. It works! (or Call Now!)

Over $X per month, and it's NOT: online marketing, day trading, FOREX, selling on eBay or any of the usual suspects. Call me at 212 234 3234 to hear a 2 min message revealing how I do it. It works! (or Call Now!)

A lead generation system that actually works! We're building our team effort-lessly. You need to learn how... Call me at 212 234 3234 to hear a 2 min message revealing this secret. It works! (or Call Now!)

I discovered a way that makes by MLM recruiting easy. Hint: you're holding half the clue. For the other half, Call me at 212 234 3234 to hear a 2 min message revealing the secret. It works! (or Call Now!)

From a networking reject to a MLM success – really – me! Now I never run out of leads, and it's NOT online! Call my 24 hr 2 min message to learn how you can too. 1 212 492 3023 – It works!

I was a failed networker – I could never find anyone to prospect - until I used this method. Now I never run out of leads, and it's NOT online! Call my 24 hr 2 min message to learn how you can too. 1 212 492 3023 – It works!

FYI, I'm a real person, and I have finally found a way to earn $4000 per month – part time – in networking. I don't do anything 'online' – that's why it works. Call my 24 hr 2 min message to learn how you can too. 1 212 492 3023 – It works!

Lead with the product messages:

I lost 27 pounds on this great new product, so can you! I've finally found some-thing that really works. I'm a real person. Call my 24 hr 2 min message to learn how you can too. 1 212 492 3023 – It works!

I was a diet junkie until a friend shared a secret with me. I lost 10 lbs in x days! Call my 24 hr 2 min message to learn how this secret can melt away/slim you too. 1 212 492 3023 – It works!

I finally beat 'mental fog'. Ever since I took this product I'm finally energetic and alert. I'm a real person. Call my 24 hr 2 min message to learn how you can too. 1 212 492 3023 – It works!

I feel like I'm 37 again! And I'm over 60! (Change ages for yourself). All it took was this amazing new method. It worked so well, I wanted to share it with you. Call my 24 hr 2 min message to learn how it can do the same for you. 1 212 492 3023 – It works!

Your 24 hour message

You need a two to 4 minute message about your opportunity. Now, readers of my other books will know to go to my book MLM Script Treasury Not Your Usual Network Marketing Phone Scripts http://www.amazon.com/Treasury-Network-Marketing-Scripts-ebook/dp/B00CKC5F38   to pick from many to adapt to their needs.

I can't write all your messages for you, as they can be specific about your products, or your opportunity. Having said that, most people are looking for leadership first, and opportunity/products second. So, if you can lead them past their problems, i.e. lack of leads, or learning 'how' to make MLM work for them, you will get a prospect. I have made one of these for you.

Before I get to it, some other information:

One thing to remember is timing. About 130 words equals one minute of voice so you need to consider how long your message will be if you are leading ONLY with your lead generation method – postcards – or a combo of your product and postcards.

One thing I will suggest is this, if you are writing your own message, add something about your lead generation method or about some kind of system that people can follow.

Cover how you are successful because of your postcard system, especially if your message on the card was about the lead generation. Take some from my example below.

At this point I think you should be able to write a 3 to 4 minute hotline message outlining the WIIFM (What's In It For Me) points of your opportunity, income testimonials of either yourself or what others are earning in your company – (that is the difference of using 'I' or 'we' in your message). However, I don't want to leave you hanging here, in case you don't have any idea of what to say, and I'll provide you with a good generic example based around the system, as it's the only common point we all share.

This one is easy to customize, I have provide more than you need, so you can take out some, to fit it down to 3 to 4 minutes. 3 minutes is about perfect, over 4 is too much.

Congratulations, you have just proved postcard marketing works! The fact you made this call shows that offline marketing is more powerful today than wasting time and money trying to find leads on the Internet.

Maybe you have been down the same road I've been - attempted many different methods to make money from home, from trying to figure out day trading, maybe eBay, internet marketing, network marketing, setting up websites, affiliate products, whatever. Well for me, none of that worked.

In the past, I had tried network marketing, but you know the hardest part is finding customers or finding people interesting in joining your network marketing company.

Still, everywhere I looked, I read about people making money in networking, and for the most part the products were high quality, not like the scammy stuff I found on the net.

I wanted to try networking again, but I had no way to get leads in order to prospect and build a team. Running ads? Forget it. Buying leads online? A huge waste of money and time.

And you know the really sad part was?...I found a network marketing company with a really great product that I truly believed in.

But still I had the same problem: how to find INTERESTED people?

Well, I found the solution, and I'll share it with you.

I'm part of a team that has cracked the code of finding all the people we need to talk to about earning over $4000, or much more, per month from home, in our network marketing program. (you can also say 'I'm leading a team...")

Now, as a FYI, postcards are not something our MLM company does, it's just something my/our team does. We are doing things a little differently in our team I/we teach people this postcard system in my team. You can forget about talking to your friends and family, or buying leads on the internet or becoming a telemarketer. No, we have our own proprietary method, which partly involves postcards and that makes prospecting and recruiting a breeze. You don't need to involve your computer at all!

Mind you, while we find our prospects offline, and communicate with them at first with postcards, we do use all of the modern tools on the Internet to do everything else. I guess you can say, we have found an endless ocean of good quality people like you, sick and tired of being lied to about 'internet leads' who want to build up a solid residual income in networking. The funny thing is, the computer is what makes this system work so well: people are sick of it.

If you are ready to learn about this proprietary method, which is for my/our team only, and learn about the great product I'm associated with, leave your name and number at the beep. And, for the record, we are NOT selling you postcards or a postcard training/recruiting system, but we'll share it with you - we ONLY promote our network company through our postcard system - in other words, we believe in integrity!

Now, I have given you more than you need, so you can edit it down. It's generic enough for you to use as is, or to take out some and add your own.

The only thing you'll need now is a voice mail service. Get one that you can easily share with your team. For example, when you call to enquire about the service ask if you can record your 3 or 4 minute message, and if you refer someone else, can you have YOUR message also copied over to their voice mail box, this way, if your new recruit wants the same message in your voice, it's as easy as asking for it.

This means you can have your new person up and running fast, plus, when your new person is following up with people who left their message, they can say, 'would you like to hear from the person who set this all up?', and you can be three-way'd in. Of course the prospects hear the same voice that was on the original message and that is impactful.

You can also make a digital recording and forward it by email to some voice mail providers. It depends on the company you chose. There are free or low cost no frills services like http://www.simplevoicebox.com or you can pay more.

You need to get one with an outgoing message length that will hold your 3 to 4 minute message. That is the main difference between what your home/smart phone voice mail offers and what a voice mail provider offers.

By now you are set.

You have your postcards, you know how to make your cards appear handwritten, and you know what to say on your cards.

I know that as you use this method, you'll learn and test more, and adapt what I have shown you, and refine it to your needs more and more.

Postcards work, and by combining smart database mass marketing (your mailing list), with personalization (the appearance of YOUR handwriting), you can build massively. The fact that those you recruit by this system will follow this system makes it a massive leverage winner.

You'll leverage your time and effort the way networking was meant to be!

If you have not read my other books, I'm sure you'll find them very useful. I write as I taught, and deliver information that can change your MLM business success.

Best of success!

David Williams

How to Recruit Doctors into your MLM or Network Marketing team by showing them a NO Warm Market System

http://www.amazon.com/Recruit-Doctors-Network-Marketing-ebook/dp/B00CCPZ7Z4

Where to Find Doctors – It's not where you think

A new source of Doctors (medical) who are not busy

Perfect for the Wellness Industry

No buying Leads

Not working the phone

This book is going to teach you an amazing system to recruit Doctors and an amazing system for you to build a huge, profitable and unstoppable leg under them - without the Doctor using any of their warm market, 'buying leads' or touching the phone!

Full Discloser: This is a short book. It's less than 50 pages long. It contains no fluff or padding. It's direct and to the point. The system contained is worth hundreds of thousands of dollars in sales, and could retire you. Really. Forget the low price of $8.99, forget the number of pages. This book will show you a fool proof system that ANY one can follow to build an unstoppable MLM Network Marketing business by recruiting Doctors. I have made it newbie friendly, but those with experience will take this system and put into practice very quickly.

This book will cover, step by step, and in very detailed and specific language:

How to recruit Doctors

The 'invisible' secret source of Doctors without a practice that are begging for something like what you will be able to show them

How to recruit busy Doctors with a practice and zero time

How to avoid the 'I don't want to go to my contacts/warm market' objection because you will be teaching them a system that requires ZERO warm market

And No 'buying leads'!

How to fill, yes FILL, meeting rooms with prospects all eager to join and try your products

NO conference calls, webinars, websites, Fanpages, autoresponders etc.

This is the full system, from the free ads you will place to the words on the marketing material you will print. This approached is very inexpensive to follow, quick and easy to implement, and very straight forward.

Also included are the phone scripts and person to person scripts you need to use when speaking to the Doctors, their receptionists, and to use in getting the appointment.

Forget all the 'usual suspects' techniques, this is not about dropping off DVDs, inviting them to conference calls, or creating special 'Doctors only' presentations. Forget all of that, and forget all of your old scripts and ads.

This system works for Doctors and requires NO Warm Market – I know I said that above, but it's very important you know this.

You don't need any paid advertising, Facebook, Internet, Twitter etc., this is all offline, local, and affordable.

No one has taught you this before. Guaranteed.

I'm going to show you where to get Doctors and how to approach them. This book will reveal to you a hidden world of Doctors who are not busy. I am going to share with you this source, give you all the scripts, the ads, the marketing materials, right down to what to say in the low cost marketing material.

MLM Script Treasury: Not Your Usual Network Marketing Phone Scripts

http://www.amazon.com/Treasury-Network-Marketing-Scripts-ebook/dp/B00CKC5F38

By David Williams

This book is full of the top pulling, most valuable and very rare MLM phone scripts that have earned their users many hundreds of thousands of dollars. I will say right now, the material in this book is NOT 'newbie' friendly. These scripts are for pros. If you don't know what you're doing this book is not for you.

-Turn your prospects voice mail into a recruiting machine! 12 scripts which you can customize

-What do I say to make sure my prospects watch's my DVD or online presentation?

-What is a GAP line and why you should use one, and what to say on it.

-How to take your prospects pulse

-Top Tier Phone scripts – rare and valuable – and great to modify for your own phone scripts

-What to say to get your prospect on to a conference call

-How to close your prospect after a conference call – lots of trial closes, hard closes, and objection handlers

-Common objections and how to turn them back into closing questions

I have chosen scripts that I know you will NOT find in other script books for sale, or the free PDFs that float all over the Internet. The scripts contained here are the kind of scripts that only the top leaders in a program have access to and it usually requires someone to be invited to join their inner team to gain access to them.

This book is full of very hard hitting powerful scripts that have been used by many top prospectors and closers. You can use this book to build your own scripts by modifying what you find here.

-Scripts to get a prospect to commit to a live conference call

-The hardest closing questions from the industry

-Ads that will get your Voice Mail full, and what to say on your Voice Mail screener – lots of screeners and out bound messages

-What to say to your prospect AFTER the conference call

-Voice Scripts to 'wake up the dead' – get your inactive distributors active again

-Starting your own MLM or Team Call? Need a conference call script? – 4 full conference call scripts inside

-Are you a company trainer? Do you do many trainings? Are your people dying on the phone?

If you are a trainer, a serious upline, on your way to being a player, a 'big dog', this book is for you. If you are putting together your own scripts, calls, establishing your own team, or your own network marketing company – invest in this book. Inside this book you will find: hard hitting, hard closing power calls, what to say when you reach a prospects voice mail, screeners, actual company conference calls, GAP line messages and some special bonuses to get your phone ringing plus much, much more. It's all here.

What is in this book can take a serious player to the next level.

This is most definitely an 'insider's book'.

http://www.amazon.com/Autoresponder-Messages-Network-Marketing-ebook/dp/B00D38WD38

This book contains a professionally written email drip campaign of 30 powerful, engaging and entertaining persuasive email/autoresponder messages focused on your prospects 'Financial Woes' and how YOU can help your prospect solve them.

Warning!

If you have been in Network Marketing for any length of time, you probably have accumulated a list of prospects and their email address. However, many of these prospects have entered the 'witness protection program'. In other words, they never call back or reply to your emails. Most people forget about this list, but there is GOLD in it!

Now, you probably have an email system you pay for that is filled with 'canned' autoresponders about your company, or even some generic versions to send to your list. Sometimes this is part of your 'backoffice'.

But, have you read these autoresponders being sent in your name?

They suck.

Here's why:

You have a prospect who is looking to solve THEIR problem, which is lack of money. They need money, income, some light at the end of the tunnel, cash, maybe some dough to save their home... BUT they are NOT shopping for a MLM company, an INDUSTRY, or how long your company has been in business, or even what your product does...NO... they are desperate for a SOLUTION to their problems!

But if all the emails you send out are about 'the company, the timing, the industry...or how someone else is making money – no wonder they don't bother responding to you!

Can you imagine sending emails to starving children with stories about the kids in your family that have so much food... that they're fat? Of course not. So why send emails to financially struggling people about how others are rich?

Your prospect doesn't care about other people's wealth when THEY are broke and in financial pain. In fact, it works the other why. Resentment, suspicion, distrust.

Their mind is on their lack of money and they are worried.

They are awake all night worrying about their debt because they are in financial trouble.

And what? You send them an email about how old your company is?

It's basic marketing folks; offer your prospect a solution to their problem, and relate to them on their terms.

At this point, all your prospect is interested in is finding 'a way to earn money'.

NOTE *** If you are new and have not earned a respectable income, chances are your upline will tell you to borrow someone else's story, but doing that only begs the question from your prospect– 'well, if everyone else is making money in your company, why aren't you?'

Forget that.

So, what is in this book? Do I teach you how to write emails? NO…NO…and NO!!!!

Is this some lessons on basic copy writing for MLM? Heck NO!!!

But let's face it. Most people can't write a note to save their lives, let alone a well-crafted email campaign. Forget learning a skill that will take you years to master – just use expert messages instead!

That's where this book of powerful 'financial woes' autoresponder messages will come to your aid.

Inside are 30 rock solid emails that focus on your prospects financial situation - with engaging humor and playfulness - showing how YOU and your program can help him out of his or her financial mess.

FULL DISCLOUSER – this is a small book – 30 powerful emails. You are not paying for the quantity of words, you are paying for the quality of the message and for getting your phone to ring.

This book contains 30 well-crafted powerfully written emails that and fun and engaging that will suggest and reinforce to your prospect that YOU are the answer to their financial problems using proven psychological and persuasion techniques.

Take these email autoresponder messages and enter them into your backof-fice or your email program. Start dripping on your list with these professionally written email messages – each crafted to have your prospect motivated to reach out and call YOU as an answer to their Financial Woes!

OVER 150 THE SIMPLEST, SHORTEST, MOST POWERFUL MLM AND NETWORK MARKETING PROSPECT CONTROL AND CLOSING LINES AND SCRIPTS, EVER.

DAVID WILLIAMS

http://www.amazon.com/Network-Marketing-Online-Professional-ebook/dp/B00DVCTK78

Do you have trouble closing prospects? Do you feel you lose control of your prospecting and follow up calls? Do you have trouble closing strong prospects – the very ones you desperately want on your team?

Well, this book is for you. It's the lowest price but highest value book on Amazon. Why? Because this little book contains over 120 of the strongest, easiest, subtlest closing and 'keeping control' and 'taking control' over the conversation lines for network marketers.

FULL DISCLOSURE: This is a short book. This book has over 150 'lines'; mostly one line sentences. But don't be fooled by the size of the book. These are powerful closing lines to allow you to close your prospect. This is NOT a book on prospecting, recruiting or even a script book.

This is a book that should be open at your desk as you make your prospecting and follow up calls. If you find you prospect off their script (they never stay on script – only you can do that), these lines will bring you back into control.

They are subtle, but powerful. Here's some samples:

How much does it cost?

Millions of dollars not to get involved

Can you see yourself taking people through a process just like I did with you?

You can't outsource your learning

The table's set

This is thick

I'm not claiming we have an automatic system, I'm demonstrating it

Get into the game with us

Let me layout how the business will start for you

This is just a process to see if there a fit for you

This is not a pressure gig

It's just the way we do this (process)

There's no glory in paying bills

I promise I'm not going to push you, chase you or sell you

I'm not going to come back to close you, but to personalize the business for you

NOTE: with very little modification, you can use many of these lines as ad headers, email subject lines, or as smart and directed text in emails or create new phone scripts or reinvigorate old ones.

Now, you don't have to memorize these lines, you just need to have your Kindle reader, iPad or even your Kindle for PC open, (or you can print out the pages), when you are making your calls. If you lose control of a conversation, or have a strong person on the line (the best kind to recruit), these 'lines' are the arrows in your quiver.

Make these lines your own. They have been collected by professionals and have earned those who have used them millions of dollars, no exaggerating, millions of dollars. Now for .99 cents they are yours.

This book of powerful network marketing closing and control lines provides you with the easiest way to sound strong on the phone. You just need to use them. You need to sound strong. Your prospect will never know what hit them until you are training them, and tell them to pick up this little book.

If they won't spend .99 cents, to get a copy, they aren't worth your time. If they ask you to make them a copy instead, they have just told you they are not worth your time. You now own this book, make these lines your own, become powerful and rich.

You do deserve it!

Printed in Germany
by Amazon Distribution
GmbH, Leipzig